SHINE
WITHOUT
AUTHORITY

JEANETTE ORTEGON

Dedication

For Shirley, who did the best she
could with what she was given.

Table of Contents

Preface

Before writing this book, I asked myself what makes me so qualified to write a book on leadership? What makes my take on leadership so different from all the other authors who wrote leadership books? Well, I do know that one of the jobs of a leader is to develop skill-sets in other people. I am not sure if there's anything so different, maybe just the way I decided to tell my story. See, I did not have many examples of leadership growing up.

My mom had been incarcerated more than half my life by the time I joined the Navy at the age of twenty-one. Because of her poor decision making and drug use, my sister, brother, and I grew up sleeping on my aunt's sofa bed or any spot that was available on the floor. My mother was not a dumb woman; she allowed bad men to negatively influence and manipulate her. My sister and I discuss all the time that if she had channeled her energy to positive things, she could have been a doctor, a lawyer, a judge or followed a career path of her choice. My aunt already had 13 children of her own in a three-bedroom, one-bathroom house and when her sister found herself in prison, she had to find a way to take in her three kids —my sister and brother and me.

I grew up in the heart of South Central Los Angeles, Compton, and Watts and did not find anything abnormal about walking through the projects everyday going to school. The lack of leadership in my life as a teenager led me to my own devices. I had no mentors; I had no community. I only had myself—and God, of course. So I made some bad decisions that nearly cost me my life. The doctor told my sister I coded at the age of 17 and after saving me, he counted me as one of his miracles. But God said, *No, not yet; she has a purpose.* My love for God is the only thing that kept me fighting for an identity, a seat at the table.

The only father figure I had growing up was my uncle Joe. He was a minister and he would take us to church on Sunday morning, Sunday evening, and Wednesday evening for Bible study. My mother was incarcerated throughout my entire middle school and high school years. I did not have someone to sit down with me and help me with my homework; no one told me how to protect myself as a young woman. As I mentioned, my aunt had 13 other children so the additional three from her sister were an added burden. I did not really feel loved growing up. I always felt like my sister and I were in the way. We were an addition to someone else's life.

God protected us throughout that entire time from some ugly things that can happen to children who grow up in the system. We were able get through unscathed because God had a purpose for both of us. I always felt that God allowed us to see and experience just enough to make sure we would never go down that path. We were exposed to just enough that we didn't indulge and fall into the street traps that everyone else did. It deterred my sister and me from the desire to do wrong. I now understand his providential plan required us to experience and go through what we had to go through in "that house." I guess I should be thankful that my aunt took us in; we could have been separated through the foster care system, landed in a group home for several years or any other horrible possible outcome.

More than anything, I thank my aunt for raising us in the church. But why does all this make me care so much about leadership? Is it because I did not have good leaders growing up? Is it because I witnessed bullying by senior officers during my time in the Navy? Maybe the seeds were being planted. I observed behaviors that were not right, and I knew I had to fight for change. But what really intrigued me about leadership is the experiences I have encountered from working for horrible bosses (I dare not refer to them as leaders). I had a front row seat into the life of some of the most treacherous people. These experiences helped me see what "not to do" and what "to do" as a leader. I enjoy helping people! I really want to inspire people to keep going. I want to show people that THE dead end is not THE end. Change the course; it is never too late to turn around.

Sometimes God will keep you in that situation to make you stronger. He hears your prayers, sees your anxiety and hears your daily anguish but he also knows you will get through it because he is there with you. Hard times are coming for you, and you're not going to be able to explain where they come from but one thing you should know is that God's grace is sufficient for you and he has his arms wrapped around you. There is also a scripture in the Bible that says "my grace is sufficient for you" (2 Corinthians 12:7-10). So my burning desire to speak, inspire and love comes from being exposed to some of the worst leaders created. Influence without authority is ineffective, but you must learn to shine without authority. I wanted this book to help people. I want this book to show people that there is a very narrow light at the end of your tunnel. I have committed myself to be the best leader that I possibly can be, and, in my trials, I choose to triumph.

The journey has just begun. I come from a hard upbringing. I thank God for keeping me grounded and for protecting me from myself. There have been times in my life where I knew it was the end, but God has a purpose for my life, and I want to fulfill that purpose. This journey chose me. My burning desire and passion to set an example of leadership is proof that this road is for me. I have the courage to speak about God as the servant leader that I am. I do have a voice and I thank God for the platform he has provided for me. And with that said, my personal vision is ...

- *While in my consciousness, to cultivate and promote the hidden qualities of my subordinates to prepare them to become effective leaders in the future.*

- *I will accomplish this by making readily available the necessary tools for enhancing creativity and imagination through education, exposure, growth, and personal accountability. I will create an experience that will echo throughout generations.*

- *I would like to be remembered as a servant leader who selflessly promoted the positive agenda of others before myself.*

- *I will continue to live demonstrating integrity and empathy, in order to inspire positive energy in others.*

- *I will continue to work toward mastering the art of "assuming good intention" and "never taking it personally" by seeking emotional balance through prayer and meditation.*

- *I will respect and love others to the best of my ability, offering my time, talent, and treasures to help those who are unable to help themselves, with the intention of setting an example of humility and improving the perception of those less fortunate. Overall, I will improve the interpersonal experience of those I encounter, in whatever capacity.*

Chapter 1:
Another Book on Leadership, Yes!

When I decided to write this book, I intended to express several things. First, I wanted to create awareness of the impact prayer can have on leadership. Soren Kierkegaard explained, "The function of prayer is not to influence God, but rather to change the nature of the one who prays." After reading that quote, I wanted to enthusiastically tell a story of how prayer kept me grounded when I was encircled with toxic leadership and to explain how many of the things I have been exposed to in my life helped me forgive while fighting toward resilience. In the battle for resiliency, you will need to fight to go forward. My experiences define who I am today. This book not only tells my story, but the stories of others who have also fought to go forward, regardless of whether they were a victim of toxic leadership or a leader who knew the return on investment you manifest when you put people first. Sir Richard Branson stressed that leaders should "train people well enough so they can leave, but treat them well enough so they do not want to." Not all leaders are toxic; there are many who actually care about the most undervalued asset in an organization—PEOPLE.

This is actually the third time I have started this book. Before today, I was being too cautious. I was considering what everyone else would think about the content. The one thing I wanted to avoid while writing this book was the appearance of being a victim. I am not a victim; I am victorious because I converted a negative experience into something positive by sharing my experiences with the impact of negative leadership. How hard could it be to write about leadership? However, this is a different kind of leadership story. This book does not tell you what to read or what degrees to put on your wall to become a successful leader. This book gets to the root of what makes an excellent leader.

There are certain qualities one must possess to be an extraordinary leader, and, in my experience, a healthy prayer life, empathy, and patience are at the forefront of success. In addition, leadership requires soft skills and sometimes denying yourself the liberty of being right. John Quincy Adams, the sixth President of the United States highlighted, "If your actions inspire others to dream more, learn more, do more and become more, you are a leader." Here is a quick thought on leadership: *The best leaders are born that way... They are manifested, obvious, clear, unmistakable, undeniable, noticeable, recognizable, while displaying understanding, compassion, and integrity.*

> *Let us not become weary in doing good, for at the proper*
> *time we will reap a harvest if we do not give up.*
> – Galatians 6:9 NIV

So the first attempt at writing this book just was not what readers needed to hear; it wasn't me being myself at all. I recall looking into the faces of colleagues who did not lead themselves through an open door thinking, *This is some good stuff* and by faith, I overcame those undesirable experiences and decided to share them with those who might be going through the same challenges. I feel if you are going to tell a story, you might as well tell it right the first time. I did not want my first attempt at being an author to fail. Readers can see through garbage. They know when they are not getting what they paid for. I was inspired to write this book after reading a book called *Maid*, by Stephanie Lane. She wrote a book about the dark side of being a maid while receiving government assistance, so she could support her infant daughter. If she was courageous enough to include all the grim details about her personal life and work experiences, I am willing to share my experiences about leadership. This book is about encouragement in motivation; it is a must read for good or bad leaders. If you are going to be responsible for someone's livelihood 40 hours a week, you should at least know how to treat them and how to improve their experience while they are working toward making you look good.

After completing the first few chapters, I realized my book was going in the wrong direction. The book *Maid* was vulnerable, and it threw it all out there the first time. I thought, *Well, she feels she has nothing to gain by holding back the truth.* It was a great book. The most important thing about writing a book on any subject is being truthful. Someone needs to hear what you've experienced, and they need to know how you got through it, which I attribute to my faith in God. So in a courageous attempt to build my street cred as an inspiring author and resilient speaker, I give to you a story of inspiration and influence and how it can all be shattered at a moment's notice.

So here goes—the servant leader will take you to school on the do's and don'ts of leadership. I am sharing it all in hopes of helping those who are struggling with negativity similar to what I struggled with. Through the explicit recounting of my pain, along with stories I have heard along the way, I pray you find your way to peace and contentment. I pray that you can forgive your oppressors, not only in the workplace, but every damaging spirit that has entered your life. What I am NOT going to do is beat you with my religious beliefs, I am going to explain how prayer combined with faith has worked for me. If you never stepped into a church a day in your life, everybody believes in prayer and everyone has called on God, whether it was at the doctor's office, before the interview, before swiping the credit card or writing the check. Everyone who believes that God exists believes that he listens when they call out his name. I challenge you today to take from my experiences and learn how God listens and how he will be there when you need him. There is an old saying: "God is not always there when you call, but he is always on time." Another opportunity for growth is what he gave me when he sat me in that valley. The enemy did not harm me or kill me; the enemy grew me. I have the success stories to prove it, and I am sure you do too. At least you will after reading this book. I hope you get everything you need from this book. I hope it gives you the courage to forgive but never forget, to be the learning leader that aligns you with success, to be the example others need to see. I know you have it in you. I had it in me but needed to work on myself so that I could see it evolve. I am so grateful that I get to share my experiences with you. My prayer is that everything you read in this book benefits you. I hope it makes you a great leader, even if you are not in a leadership position. I hope it helps you discover what a great leader should be, if and when you decide to step into that role.

Going back to why this book on leadership is different than any other book on leadership, I previously mentioned my approach to becoming a successful leader is based on prayer and if that did not scare you away, I take it you are still reading so I will continue. I have learned to pray for horrible people, which led me to believe prayer time should be on every leadership calendar. This book did not evolve overnight; it comes from years of observing the negative impact bad leadership can have on the "good guys." I am not speaking from a place of perfection; I am speaking from a place of personal growth, pain, hurt, and resiliency. My experiences have led me through a transition from run over to resiliency. My prayer life is better, I am a better manager and I am a better coach and mentor because of my fight to become. But one thing I am not: I am not a perfect person. I am not judging anyone for what they don't know or have the capability to become. And when I say judging for what they don't know, some people just don't know how to be leaders. They're kind of forced into a position based on a need to fill a gap. I am sharing more; I am open and honest with my story in hopes of giving you something that will help you overcome whatever it is you are going through.

Chapter 2:
Lacking Leadership

When the righteous are in authority, the people rejoice;
but when a wicked man rules, the people groan.
---Proverbs 29:2 NKJV

Dealing with difficult people through civility is an important part of mastering leadership. Being raised in South Central Los Angeles, I tend to say what is on my mind. I tend to stand up for myself to prevent ridicule or manipulation. Over the years, I have learned how to listen more and speak less. My mom would always say, "Let go and let God."

"The Righteous will not be forsaken"
– Psalm 37:25

One major observation that I have made on my journey is that people do not leave jobs, they leave people. When I think of horrible leaders I have met in the past, I think about all the hard-working individuals that have been forced out of good career opportunities because of toxic environments. How many innocent families have been destroyed? How many threw in the towel and just refused to take it anymore? The real impact may never be known. The worst thing is that management often refuses to remove these toxic leaders for fear of a gap in productivity. It is never about the people; it is always about the numbers and the bottom line. I attribute my successful leadership approach to the natural ability to influence people. I am good at managing people, while some managers are better at managing things. But things are not people and should not be treated the same. You are going to hear that phrase throughout this book—"managing things and not people"—because I cannot emphasize enough the importance of separating people from things.

I have always thought of myself as a servant leader. I go out of my way to make sure people have all the tools necessary to be the best future leaders they can. I strive to empower; I give the little guy an opportunity to show what he can do. It is never about me, and when we make it about "me," we fail others and ourselves. I want to be the best to everyone that I can. I do not consider myself a "know it all" leader. I enjoy learning from subordinates. I think of myself as the mayor: I work for the people. I am always collecting knowledge from those who are junior or subordinate. If I cannot do the work of everyone else, then I should be open to learning and trusting my subordinates to do what they were hired to do. It is a beautiful thing to see a flower blossom.

It is no secret that middle management can destroy an organization. If issues and concerns from subordinates are not disseminated up the organizational chain and information from senior leadership is not communicated down the chain, leadership has failed. Why should the subordinate be exempt from receiving valuable information? The best way to show impartiality to your employees is to give them a sense of ownership. Giving ownership is sharing information and paving the way for expressing new ideas. What good does it do anyone if you keep vital information to yourself? "Knowledge is power," according to School House Rock.

> *The challenge of leadership is to be strong but not rude,*
> *be kind but not weak, be bold but not a bully, be thought-*
> *ful but not lazy, be humble but not timid, be proud but not*
> *arrogant, have humor but without folly.*
> – Jim Rohn

While my mom was still on this earth, she would always tell my siblings and me, "Prayer changes things." I have used prayer for many different situations, including the day I buried her. I prayed that God would help my siblings and me get over the pain and disbelief that she was no longer with us. I prayed for the peace that passes all understanding. I used the same approach in the workplace—the peace that passes all understanding, not just in death but while in my trials, facing unexplained rejection and undeserved mistreatment, including the flying knives that had not landed yet. I endured! It was not easy, but I endured whatever was on the menu for the day. I would pray to God and thank him for the opportunity to grow, but I would also find myself asking forgiveness for failing as a Christian. I stopped praying for my oppressors.

> *And the peace of God, which surpasses all understanding,*
> *will guard your hearts and your minds in Christ Jesus.*
> – Philippians 4:7 NKJV

The more I found myself dealing with a difficult situation on the job, the harder I would pray about it. I would send fervent petitions, believing I would get an answer. Almost instantly, it seemed, I could see the situation correcting itself. But as I reflect, maybe it was me who changed and not my circumstances. A good attribute of a leader is showing vulnerability and patience. Brené Brown, the *mother of vulnerability* research, says, "You cannot be hard as stone and expect people to learn from you." It is a must that you show yourself as a leader. Share yourself so your cohorts can learn from you. What a beautiful gift of generosity.

I rebuked any negative thought that resembled a victim. When you're dealing with self-hating people, you look at them and think, *Dang! Somebody did a number on them.* I do not think people necessarily have a poster board of victims they target; they only carry over the hurt that was done to them. They swallow it into their own spirit. They were never able to get over it; they lived, breathed, and ate it all day.

As a leader you must have good interpersonal skills. Many leaders or those who believe themselves to be leaders based on their title, lack interpersonal skills. There was one special employee in my organization who was an extreme introvert. This employee would stare at the wall while engaging in a full conversation before he would look you in the eye. Based on his level of subject expertise, the ongoing discussion from top leadership was to put him in a leadership role, which would require that he interact with people daily. That would have been a train wreck for this employee because he barely spoke to anyone—and now management wanted to forcefully elevate his nonexistent interpersonal skills? But the focus was never on the employee, the focus was on the need of the organization. Based on other requirements, that idea was buried without implementation. Being in a position of influence without authority is tough. I would have never introduced that idea. All I could do was to sit back, and watch a life-changing decision being made about someone who had no buy-in or say-so. It is painful to watch people suffer and be unable to jump in to help them. You cannot convince me that seeing these behaviors firsthand would not make anyone a better leader. My current atmosphere is a great learning experience for me. I am in my valley, but I do see the peak. I always remember that in order to prepare you for the next level, God will keep you in your circumstances so that you can grow. Dipped in hot gold!

During my leadership teaching moments, I enjoy viewing motivational videos on social media. I read about brilliant leaders who strive to make a difference in the lives of random people on a daily basis. One of the interesting things I have learned is that every successful leader has a story of adversity and despair. Seconds before the house explodes, just before the car runs over the cliff, there is a success turning point. It's always that one moment of despair that gets the adrenaline pumping. For example, Tyler Perry is one of the greatest inspirations to humanity. As a leader and entrepreneur, he has opened the door for so many minorities to gain success in the film industry. I watched an interview he did with Oprah Winfrey where he explained how every circumstance was a teaching moment from God. He describes how for several years his theatre plays failed, regardless of how much time and money he invested. But he did not give up; he kept believing that a breakthrough was inevitable as long as he kept his faith in God. When he did blossom into success, the obstacles became greater; the fight was on a much larger scale. Tyler Perry succeed in the theatre, now it was time to test the big screen. This time, he brought more to the table. With his first-ever success in theatre, Hollywood had no choice but to take him seriously. I'm sure there were naysayers but confidence along with a great track record spoke for itself. We all know how that story ends—continues, actually.

For I know what plans I have for you, declares the Lord,
plans to prosper you and not to harm you, plans to give
you hope and a future.
– Jeremiah 29:11 NIV

God has transformed me into the person I need to be, setting me up for his providence. I was being prepared for elevation. I prayed fervently, and I think leaders should pray. Leaders should pray for their employees, pray for themselves, pray for patience, and pray for their careers. God should always be involved in anything you take seriously. That includes health, finances, security and especially our leaders and subordinates. I am not the first one who decided to use prayer as a defense mechanism, but I chose to write about it because prayer is something that is so overlooked and can be so powerful. I attest!

Now that I am in a position of influence and I have an impact on the professional lives of others, I need to be mindful of the example I am setting. I have experienced heartache after heartache. I had to hold on to my faith and believe the situation would change. I have never been one to retaliate, but that is exactly what I did. You do not want to speak to me, then I am not speaking to you. Tit for tat is so childish. That is what happens when you go back and forth, basically returning bad behavior to the one who gave it to you. That does not get you anywhere. A job must be done, and the most civil thing is choosing a peaceful approach. For me that was prayer. My deepest prayers were asking God to change my situation, but I said, "God, if I have to go through this turmoil, change me so that I see it differently, according to your will." And I started seeing things differently. Now that I think about it, I have always asked God to change me so my circumstances would change. Your reaction to any negative situation thrown your way is based on how you see it. I never stopped praying for the enemy, which is one of the hardest things to do—pray for someone that has intentionally inflicted harm upon you.

Case Study #1:
Authority is Only a Label

"Now you see it, now you don't," "what's here today is gone tomorrow," "in one hand and out the other"—just a few thoughts that come to mind when I hear the word authority. It is only a title that can be stripped away at any time. Depending on your career field, dethroning does not need much justification, hence the title of this book. Authority does not necessarily mean power over people. It can mean overseeing a thing or a process. As a leader in my organization, it can be nerve-racking to constantly wonder about the outcome of my daily fate. What chaos awaits me today? What battles do I accept and what do I leave on the table?

I recently attended a leadership training course that required students to complete a DISC assessment. Dominance (D), Influence (I), Steadiness (S), Conscientiousness (C) is an assessment tool that provides insight to help an individual understand their behavioral differences when interacting with others. There are four sections to the DISC assessment. "D" for Dominance, "I" for Influence, "C" for Conscientiousness, and "S" for Steadiness. It had been a few years since I completed my last assessment and I was curious to see how I fared this time around. It was interesting to see that I was still in the influential and steadiness categories. Other students in the class were either high "D" or low "C," etc. I immediately took offense to the high "D" group, because one of my most horrific supervisors was a high "D" without seeing his assessment—I just felt it. It wasn't fair to paint this particular group with the same brush as an atrocious supervisor, but it was hard to witness this particular group of "D" people delight in being dominant to a compassionate group of people, especially a group that worked so hard for them. I guess I took it personally. I thought about how hard I worked for toxic bosses and how hard they worked to keep me minimized. Subordinate relationships are ruined because bosses fail to endorse their managers on major decisions. Subordinates sensed I had no real authority and drove right past me to get an approval from my boss. There were times when people would enter the office and ask for the boss. When I explained that he was not available, instead of explaining the situation to me, they would just say, "OK I'll come back later" without giving me the opportunity to address their needs. It can be hurtful when you put so much effort into being a great leader but are continually reduced.

Colin Powell, a retired four-star general and the first African-American Secretary of State, said, "Leadership is solving problems. The day soldiers stop bringing you their problems is the day you have stopped leading them." After reflecting on this quote, I began to think maybe I'd failed my people. No one came to me for support. Then I immediately thought of my level of influence that remained in place. My subordinates would approach me for career advice and promotion package reviews. We would have lunch or meet up for happy hour. So once again referring to the title of this book, influence without authority showed itself to be relevant. When an employee is seeking on-the-job support, it is only to meet a specific requirement that is in the moment, temporary, a one-and-done. Those instances are important for promotion opportunities, as well. But when a subordinate meets you on a personal level, that is a sign of influence and servant leadership. Influential relationships outlast authoritative relationships. Authoritative relationships have expiration dates; influence lasts a lifetime. I had to change my definition of what I thought leadership was. It is hard to gain traction as a leader if you are not supported by your leadership. A leader's number one responsibility is to grow more leaders, and in many cases that means standing behind your second in command, even if you do not 100% agree with their decisions. You may pull them aside and have a discussion, but in the presence of subordinates, you always support your managers 100%. To remain successful as a leadership team, the manager must validate the assistant to maintain relevance in the eyes of other employees. It is kind of like running to Dad when Mom says no, Dad has to say no too, in order to maintain stability within the household.

A true test of my leadership ability always happened when my leadership was unavailable. It seemed almost like clockwork, but I knew it was God's providence allowing me the opportunity to shine without interference. The worst emergencies would happen that required me to step up as the single leader of the organization. And I can say those were the best opportunities for me to display my leadership abilities without distractions. All decisions were made by me, all subordinates reported to me, and in most cases, I was able to gain support from the most qualified resources without admitting I needed help. I could influence without asking. This was also the best opportunity for me to bond with my subordinates. We had a chance to learn about each other and get to know each other better when the leadership was not involved. I had more face-time with senior executives and was able to grow professionally in areas

I was not regularly privy to. I knew once the boss returned, I would revert back to the position of assistant, praying that my influence would have been impactful enough to keep me relevant.

Influence without authority is not a leadership failure. Influence has the capacity to survive authority and can inspire rather than torment subordinates. The more I put the negativity behind me, the more God answered that old prayer, "Lord, give me the opportunity to serve others; use me to do your will." All of a sudden the big projects would come my way. Many thought I was not able to handle projects of such magnitude, but I grabbed the bull by the horns. I was able to run the most complex projects error-free. They required me to coordinate with many associations throughout different geographical locations. I summoned the smartest people I had under my purview. I have always believed you do not need to have all the answers; you do need to know where to get the answers. That is where you rely on the talent of your team to do what they were hired to do. A great leader does not have all the answers or pretend that they do. Leaders should be willing to learn from their subordinates. The day I transferred from the organization, all I could think about were the smart and talented people that helped me become successful at doing my job. I never thought I got there on my own. I always gave praise to the team members who did their job with such professionalism and made my job easy. That was influence at its finest.

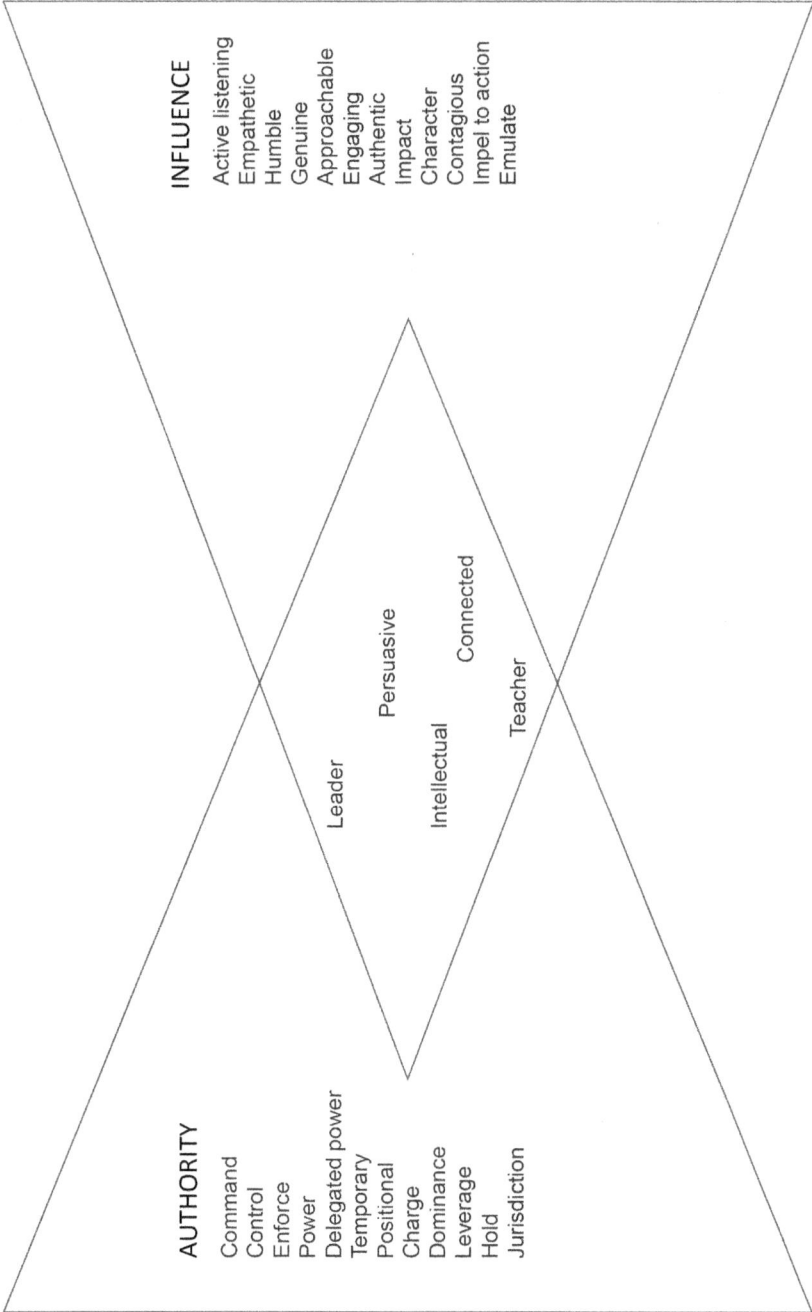

INFLUENCE

Active listening
Empathetic
Humble
Genuine
Approachable
Engaging
Authentic
Impact
Character
Contagious
Impel to action
Emulate

Connected

Persuasive

Teacher

Intellectual

Leader

AUTHORITY

Command
Control
Enforce
Power
Delegated power
Temporary
Positional
Charge
Dominance
Leverage
Hold
Jurisdiction

Chapter 3:
When There is a Rough Start... (There is a Stronger Finish)

I would like to think I knew where it all started. What created the burning desire to spread the good news on leadership? As much as I tried to be, I was never outspoken. Students in my class would take cheap shots and insults at me all the time, but I just laughed it off, hoping I would be the only one to notice they were laughing at me instead of with me. I was raised in South Central Los Angeles. Staying away from the drug dealers and the prostitutes was the daily hustle. I never bought into the "if you cannot beat them join them" philosophy. I ran! I ran home from school. I ran to school. I ran to the corner store. I ran to band practice. I ran to my friend's house. Growing up in South Central you knew how and when it was time to run. As far as I can remember, I only wanted to enjoy people's company and learn from different environments. There was not too much to learn other than how to survive in the streets, which alley to avoid on the way home from school, or which of your friend's houses was targeted as a drug house by the police. From my childhood, I remember the shock of the neighborhood when we all learned that the mentally disabled brother of one of our friends was a serial rapist who would escape his locked bedroom at night to rape and murder women. He would then dump their bodies in the back alleys or on the railroad tracks. Those kinds of things were normal growing up in Watts.

My sister, brother and I grew up in the heart of South Central, in a three-bedroom house with my aunt, uncle and their 13 children. My aunt practically raised us. My mom did not make the best decisions in life so when the eviction notices popped up on the door or my mom would get arrested, we moved in with my aunt and her family. Her living room sofa bed became amazingly comfortable to us over the years. Although my aunt had a house full of her own children, she still always found room for my siblings and me. When we lived with my mom, I remember coming home from school and seeing the padlock on the door with an eviction notice, which happened several times throughout my childhood. Just when it seemed like she got things together, another eviction notice and another night in a motel brought us back to reality. When my twin sister, brother, and I were younger, we would pump gas at the corner gas station just to get motel money for the night. I guess I can say that was my first interaction with leadership and critical thinking. Whenever we were thrown out of our apartment, my sister, brother, and I would set a goal of making $7.00 each to cover the $21.00 nightly motel fee. So I guess you could say I learned how to manage money at an early age.

My aunt Debra, who also lived in Los Angeles, would come to our rescue on many occasions. The best part of my childhood was when Aunt Debra would take us to her house in Watts during the summer. Watts was a good upbringing for me. Although it was a rough neighborhood, the summers we stayed with my extended family made us feel loved. I felt like I had a chance to have a normal childhood, without waiting in line to use the bathroom behind 13 other people. It was amazing and we always dreaded summer ending. We treasured the times when Aunt Debra would take us to the movies and our favorite family diner in Long Beach, Norms or Vasilios. Aunt Debra has always been a second mother to me. She financially supported my children during the first few years of my Navy career. I was only an E-3 and did not have enough money to take care of our needs. To this day I am thankful to God that Aunt Debra would always step in and help when my kids needed necessities such as diapers and milk. Aunt Debra was always supportive and uplifting. She never judged my mom; she only took us in and made sure we had a safe place to sleep and food on the table.

My mom was the complete opposite. She was feisty and said what was on her mind and then some. There were times when she would get into arguments with people and go from zero to a hundred within seconds, which I attribute to her early life of drug and alcohol abuse. My mom was a very emotionally driven woman. One thing I learned from her was to never let anyone take advantage of me. She did not provide the best examples, but I got a good idea of what she meant.

In school, I would avoid confrontation with anyone who was looking for trouble. In high school you always had that class clown who wanted an audience and would always seek out the weakest victims as volunteers. I was always able to diffuse tense situations through civility. Civility did not work every time, but it was always worth a shot.

Fast forward to marriage and my military career. I married young. I met my (now) ex-husband over the phone while looking for a number for the local auto parts store. He was working as a 411 operator and I thought it was weird that he flirted with me instead of giving me the number I requested. I was only 19 years old, so I fell for it. He was 31 years old and looking for a wife—his second wife, to be exact. So after one date and a few sleepovers, we ended up getting married after dating for two years. I knew this was not what I wanted, but what did I know at 19 years old? Do not get me wrong, I was in love but deep down inside, I knew that I should have not been looking for a wedding dress at 19 years old. We said "I do" in front of the Eternal Flame at the Justice of the Peace in downtown Waikiki. After the small fee of 50 dollars for the marriage certificate and a romantic meal at the food court in the local mall, we were husband and wife.

With no clear direction for my life, I made the decision to join the Navy prior to marrying the telephone operator. His name was Raul. My first duty station was in Hawaii. Serving in paradise was blissful. Being from Los Angeles, I was not unfamiliar with sandy beaches, but there was something about the ambience of being on an island far away, reflecting on how I barely escaped my life in South Central. All the mistakes I had made were separated from me by the Pacific Ocean. The military was a good choice for me. I have never been a person without discipline, but it gave me a sense of direction and it gave me a sense of purpose, along with other benefits that come with serving your country, such as an opportunity to travel the world for free. I was incredibly happy to be in the military. Within two years, I gave birth to my son. It was perfect: somebody to look after, someone to protect and impart my knowledge to. Although my husband at the time did not make the best career decisions, the military took great care of us, and we were a happy family.

My first job in the military was a tugboat operator, which was my only option since I did not score high enough on the ASVAB military entrance exam test to get a career position in the building. I did not care about the grunt work. I was out of South Central and my family was taken care of. We were living free with no worries and we were in Hawaii—how good was that?

After the birth of my daughter, things got a little shaky in my marriage. I needed Raul to help more, but he decided working was more important than family. God blessed me with so much. I soon realized I did not have a partner to raise my children WITH me. This realization lasted for several years throughout my military career; the military is not big on separating families. They make all provisions available for the families to be together, such as education and employment, providing training to service members and their families. They make everything perfect for your children, and they have the best schools and childcare resources. The military was the best environment to raise my children. The one thing they did not do was allow time and space to work on family issues. That was something I had to work through on my own. After trying to make our marriage work, I'd had enough. I was so depressed; I began to experience extremely dangerous thoughts. I threw in the towel on the marriage. With the challenges of preparing for promotion and traveling from multiple duty locations, which included overseas, I could not effectively focus on a military career with all the negative things that were going on within my personal life. I had decided to give up even though, as a Christian, divorce for unhappiness is not looked upon favorably in the church. I should have never been in that marriage, but I was only 19 years old and no one really knows what they want at that age, but they think they do. Raul was not a bad person; we were just not good together. I was so young and naive when we met, and he was in his 30s, which meant he was looking for a wife and I was trying to turn 21 and enjoy what life had to offer. We have two beautiful children and we have an amazing friendship that most people do not understand. I chuckle when I hear "why is he still living in your house? Why are you always talking to him?" One co-worker even commented, "You do not have to be loyal to your ex-husband, you know." My rationale was, why would I alienate my children from their father? The worst thing you can do is make your kids choose a side. They did not ask to be here, so I felt it was my duty as a mother to put them first, even if it meant sacrificing my wants and desires. Once they were born, many of my decisions were all about them. No one understands our complicated friendship, but we understand it and it works for us.

In 2006, I decided to leave the military and focus on a normal life for me and the kids. I was also having problems maintaining my body weight, which played a big factor in me leaving the Navy before eligibility for retirement. However, I was blessed to have been offered a position doing the same exact job but as a civilian. I had a great friendship with my first civilian boss, Sam. Sam lived in Pennsylvania and had two daughters and a beautiful wife. I thank him for introducing me to golf. I still crown him as the best leader I have ever worked for. He reminded me of my most influential military leader, Mark. Mark was my watch supervisor when I was stationed in Japan. He, like Sam, was also married with two children. He was a great guy and he loved his family, which is why he did a great job at the whole work-life balance. When I mentioned to

Sam that I was leaving the Navy, he offered me a job as a civilian. He submitted for a direct hire, so I was able to get hired at a more senior paygrade without competing with other applicants. I will never forget what he did for me.

My first civilian job was not a leadership position. I was hired as a System Administrator, which required me to constantly interact with customers more than what I was used to. It was basically the same job as my military job but allowed more freedom outside the uniform. It was a great learning experience; I got the opportunity to see firsthand what it was like to think on my own. I also learned how to keep calm when dissatisfied customers became emotionally charged. The transition from military life to civilian life was not that difficult. I went from making $25,000 a year to $85,000 a year overnight, which was a true blessing. I made some financial mistakes that eventually landed me in bankruptcy court, but God allowed me to keep my home and my job. I could have avoided financial trouble if I had been more demanding about receiving child support payments from my ex-husband. I never turned in the court papers that would have mandated him to pay through payroll deductions from the state of Maryland. I always believed child support was used as a weapon against fathers by angry mothers. I am not saying this is the case for everyone; I just remember growing up hearing family members and their friends plotting against their "baby daddy" and it always included child support as their weapon of choice. I remember some women threatening the father of their children with child support revenge even if they decided to move on with their lives, dating another nice lady from the hood. I decided to let Raul make the decision on what support he wanted to contribute to the upbringing of his children.

I eventually recovered from bankruptcy. The sudden pay increase from military to civilian was a bit overwhelming, I eventually put a solid budget in place that I adamantly followed. I did not realize how much money I did not make until I got to the closing table after purchasing my first home. The military was good for me and my family; I have no complaints. I only wish they had taught me more about finances or fiscal responsibility after leaving the military. I got it right eventually.

Case Study #2:
No Turning Back

I was asked to give a presentation on resiliency during Nurses' Week 2019. The discussion was intended to give hope and encouragement to nurses who have endured stress, anxiety and other things that go along with a fast-paced work environment. The Family Advocacy Director and the New Parents Support Program nurse were extremely impressed with my presentation. After the presentation ended, the discussion of hope and encouragement persisted when I continued the conversation with the New Parents Support Program nurse, Eun Ju Kim. Her story was very intriguing.

Eun was a Korean American who entered the Army at an early age without understanding English. She had a young daughter who was being looked after by her parents in Korea while she finished bootcamp. She overcame the communication barrier because of a photographic memory that allowed her to memorize the Army instructional training manual, and eventually she graduated from boot camp successfully. She was a combat medic and provided medical support to many soldiers during her six-year stay in the Army. The intriguing thing about her story was how a Korean immigrant migrated to America and entered one of the most difficult Armed Forces, the United States Army. Many people think *OK, people come from foreign countries and join the American military every day—what is so interesting about that?* Well, I respond by saying she did not enter the military for herself; she entered the military to provide a better life for her daughter, a sacrifice many would not even consider. She left her daughter 11,000 miles away. That decision was very risky, as she didn't even know if she was going to finish bootcamp or not because she could not understand English. Eun found herself surrounded by American battle buddies who helped her succeed. A single parent taking a chance in and unknown country just to provide a better opportunity for her daughter, elderly mother, and father, Eun would continue serving her newly adopted country in Guam and Arizona.

After a near fatal accident while riding in a paramedic vehicle, Eun was discharged from the Army. After attending nursing school in Pennsylvania, the combat medic became a registered nurse. Today, Eun continues to serve the Army at Yongsan Army Base in Seoul, Korea.

Chapter 4:
Leader in the Making

My first leadership position as a civilian was a development experience. I managed mainly a younger group of technical employees, military and civilian. There was not much one-on-one interaction. I was only responsible for scheduling their daily activities. I only stayed in that position for two years. I quickly realized there was no potential for growth, and it was a simple job that offered no possibilities for the future and I needed to do something better if I wanted my career to advance. I was way behind the curve because the first few years as a civilian involved getting through the divorce and managing the transition from the military to civilian, so many other things had seemed more important than making my way up the corporate ladder. Things that were going wrong in my personal life were a big distraction.

I eventually decided to relocate to a new office. It was not a position that I was familiar with, but I knew I needed to do something. I did not grasp the new job that easily; it was difficult for me to learn this new way of doing things. After a few months, the office manager realized that position was not for me, so she decided to relocate me to another position within the office. This is where it all began. This was the exact location when I realized what made a good leader and what made a not so good leader. This was the moment I discovered my God-given talent, the gift to unify and positively influence people. Although this was the most difficult office I have served in, it was also the most edifying. It gave me a crash course in team building and an opportunity to learn about what leadership style I wanted to adopt.

I felt my coworkers held my misfortune of being removed from my first position against me. I was judged and negatively portrayed after I was removed from my first position for poor performance. I did my best to fit in but the dark cloud over my head did not go away until I got into the groove of the new position. After several weeks it was obvious I had found my niche, interacting with other people. The previous position required me to work a process; the new position allowed me to interact with customers outside the office environment. I am a firm believer that people are not things and should not be treated as such. A process is something that is directed; a person is someone who is encouraged. I never saw myself as one who would enjoy leading in a big organization. I enjoyed one-on-one interaction and small groups. I was always quiet and did not want to make a scene until I got to this office. I was able to get up and move around and talk to people, which I really enjoyed. Walking the hallways was therapeutic. It allowed me to forget about the negativity around me.

My new position was a big success. I understood what I was doing, and I had a network of people external to my immediate workspace to help me whenever I needed assistance. I felt different inside: I was happy. I immediately shined throughout the entire office. I became a superstar overnight because of my "won't stop, cannot stop" work ethic. Well, everyone did not take so kindly to my drive and tenacity. Especially since I was more productive than the incumbent. I immediately felt resentment. I wondered if I was being targeted because I was too good at the job—a perfect example of how influence without authority can create a following of supporters that genuinely want to see you succeed, but you will always have those who cannot stomach the idea of you succeeding. Because of my infectious interpersonal skills, I created working relationships that were never imaginable. I basically arrived and changed the culture of the organization and maybe that was not appreciated by all, but should I have held back because of the insecurities of others? Was I expected to "water down" to make the naysayers feel comfortable? No, you blossom and do the best you can, especially when the opportunity presents itself. It was not the worst place in the world. I kept in close contact with coworkers from previous offices as a method of support. I developed relationships with out of office colleagues through random conversations in the hallways or anywhere I had the opportunity to strike up a conversation. That was the best thing about having an outlet: You can take your mind to a place that allows you to regroup and refocus on what really matters the most. I pause when I think that some people will hate you for the simple fact that you woke up that morning.

I started hearing conversations about how I was trying to outshine everyone. I would even get dirty looks from coworkers during meetings. I thought I had the support of leadership but quickly realized I was in a boat with no paddle in the middle of the ocean. I will never forget the response I received when I approached my supervisor requesting help with an issue I was having with another coworker, and the response was "do not worry about her, just do the job I hired you to do." In a split second, I knew I was on my own. Day in and day out the small chatter got louder and the office cliques became more noticeable. It got so bad that my health began to suffer. There were mornings when I would exit the freeway quickly and drive to the emergency room complaining of shortness of breath. I experienced several visits to the emergency room with chest x-rays, heart scans, brain scans, and anything the doctors could think of to figure out what the problem was. After several visits, the emergency physician suggested I see a therapist.

I would get to the parking lot and begin to have trouble breathing. One day it got so bad a coworker, who was also friends with the office manager, unjustly reprimanded me. As a leader, you should separate yourself from any indication of bias and nepotism. I believed my manager at the time did not support me because of influence from other people in the office. One of their best friends was my office nemesis. She was not a fan, which was fine, if she had only remained civil. She was a strong-willed older woman who did not like anyone. I had to let it be known that I was not going to take negative behavior. I got home that evening and fell to my knees and began to pray. I prayed to God that he would change the hearts of my coworkers. I prayed and asked God to help me be a better employee and I asked God to help them be softer toward me and their approach with me be gentler. Not only did this give me relief, knowing that the answer was coming soon if I just hung in there, it gave me a peace of mind knowing that none of this negative behavior was my doing. And when I say not my doing, I think to myself there was nothing that I could have done to initiate this behavior.

However, I must admit that I do have a problem dealing with conflict. I do not like conflict. I run at the sign of conflict. Since my last day in that office, I have pondered the idea of what might have happened if I had called a meeting with my supervisor and subordinates to express my discontent with the way I was being treated. Would that have eased things? Should I have spoken with my supervisor about this instead of running from it? Now that I have evolved into the leader I am today, I would speak with my supervisor to explain my concerns. That would be the leadership thing to do.

After turning to the power of prayer, I began to walk into the office with a smile on my face, being the person that I was always intended to be and not concerning myself with what anyone thought of me. You see, prayer gives you a sense of serenity. It gives you a sense of relief. It leaves you guilt-free. I mean, do not get me wrong, I had some rough days and there were days where I wanted to unleash and turn into a 300-pound silverback. I knew I had to hold my emotions together. People tend to take you to your limits on purpose, sometimes just to see how far they can push you. *DO NOT POKE THE BEAR* is all I kept thinking. I did good, for which I give credit to my military career. I served 12 years in the Navy and worked under harsh conditions from some of the most unreasonable people on the planet, but it was the military discipline that kept me intact. It really came in handy during my first year in that office. I had to put my best foot forward and make sure I stayed present for my customers. After weeks and months of praying I could see a change not only in myself, but in the people around me. There is an old saying, "You get in what you put out," so I had to make sure everything I put out was something I wanted to get in. After a few years, everything ended on a good note. I ended up making some great friends and a great mentor. Not only are these relationships long-lasting but I believe I can go back to my former colleagues when I need support or mentoring. I learned a lot from serving in that office: I learned about myself, I learned about others, and my relationship with God improved. That is because my prayer life improved. I reminisce about all those doctor's visits and co-pay fees, when all I really needed to do was pray through it. During my time in that office, I was the unhealthiest I have ever been throughout my entire life. I do not know why I stayed there for three years; I should have gotten out immediately. But I am glad I did; it was the perfect opportunity for growth and maturity. I saw a change not only in myself, but in my co-workers as well. Another added value to a leader is not running from bad situations but doing the best you can to fix relationships. It is not always worth the investment, though; some people are who they are. They have always been that way and will remain committed to zero change. I never understood why grimy people do not change, but what I did understand was that increasing my prayer life, to include praying for my enemies, would be a good indication of my growth as a leader. It is difficult to pray for those who abuse you but it is in the Bible: "Pray for those who spitefully use you and do good to those who harm you."

One of my favorite authors and pioneers of Human Resources is Mary Parker Follet. She said it best when she explained, *"Leadership is not defined by the exercise of power but by the capacity to increase the sense of power among those led. The most essential work of a leader is to create more leaders."* There are going to be times when you just need to remain flat. You're going to have to deny yourself the freedom of being right. There will be instances where you just need to put it on the shelf for a later date. Like fine wine, your emotions will have to age over time. I still remember the going-away event my office mates planned for me. One of my coworkers said, "You remind me of my own daughter." It took me back for a second because my first response was to go back to the beginning of the relationship I had with these coworkers, and I did not imagine her being any relation to me, but then I immediately diverted back to the present and decided to let the past remain in the past forever. Forgiveness is a powerful thing. It not only helps you, but it helps the other person—kind of like a trickle effect.

Case Study #3:
Captain Hulme, the People's Leader

People will forgive you for not being the leader they think you should be. People will not forgive you for not being the leader you claimed to be. – Rufus Cumberland

As an aircraft supply technician, retired Air Force Captain John Hulme shaped himself into a steward leader years before his commissioning as an Air Force officer.

John was never exposed to positive leadership; he grew up in an environment that lacked mentors. The adults in his neighborhood were suffering from alcoholism, and other self-sabotaging activities, which left him finding his own way as a teenager. His father died when he was seven years old and his sister was three months old. The best guidance he received during that time was when he attended Catholic high school, but it was still not enough to prepare him for the career that would soon follow.

At the age of 17, John decided to join the Air Force, to which he credits his resilient, confident, and structured character. During his Air Force career, John excelled at every leadership opportunity that was handed to him.

John recalls a time where he supervised a local woman at Osan Air Base in Korea, who happened to be his secretary. There were 80 personnel in his squadron, which meant little room for error. His secretary constantly made mistakes with recordkeeping, budgets, etc. Everyone in the squadron criticized her and was not happy with her performance. As a leader, John had to make a command decision that was in the best interest of everyone. He decided to remove the disastrous secretary after numerous counseling statements and written reprimands. However, in her favor, John was able to negotiate another employment opportunity for her in a neighboring squadron. Her new location had 25 personnel, which was much easier for her to manage. She came back months later to thank John for identifying she needed to make a change. She admitted that her termination was the best thing that happened to her, admitting she was not qualified to be in that position. This was a Win! Win! for everyone.

As a leader, John did not give up on his secretary. He gave her a second chance to prove her capability. Another attribute of a leader is to identify when employees are struggling and offer an alternative solution. The other side of the coin is the complete opposite. If you have an employee who is just a bad person or whatever that description of "bad" is, you need to destroy them as soon as possible. Do not throw your garbage to someone else; they will never be good anywhere they go.

John's favorite axiom, which he borrowed from a friend, was "hire slow, fire fast." Once you have identified an employee with little to no potential and whose tasks exceed their ability, make a command decision to let them go. However, John identified that his secretary had potential but was overwhelmed and needed a new position that matched her abilities. John was a firm believer in molding subordinates into future leaders by equipping them with the resources needed to become effective leaders.

While leading a squadron in Taiwan, John recognized the outstanding work ethic of a subordinate Master Sergeant. John rewarded the Master Sergeant's efforts by submitting him for promotion. Because of John's edification and quick recognition, the Non-Commissioned Officer (NCO) was promoted during the next promotion cycle. Providing subordinates with clear objectives, support, and guidance is the basic responsibility of a leader. John recognized that leaders are not always born to lead. The most successful leaders grab the brass ring and run with it.

John believed leaders needed confidence. Do not be afraid to learn from other successful leaders, including subordinates. He advised future leaders to find successful leaders and match what they do. Fortunately for potential leaders, the current competition is weak. It would be easy for successful leaders to jump right in and change the culture.

There are many stories like Captain Hulme's success with leadership. I am sure many leaders take various approaches, realizing that some will work while others will not. Do you think John prayed for his success? I am sure he did. While interviewing John, it was evident that he sought out courage in his leaders. I was glad to learn that the failing secretary was able to be relocated to another position. I am sure her experience made her more resilient. The Master Sergeant is another example of how John was able to pull greatness out of his subordinates. As a result, the Master Sergeant was promoted. Based on several other interviews that I have done for this book, it all comes down to identifying that a real leader is courageous and looks out for their subordinates.

Chapter 5:
You Cannot Always Choose Your Subordinates

The best thing about being a leader is learning how to deal with difficult situations. Interpersonal skills are particularly important on all sides: leaders, subordinates, and exterior contacts and outside organizations. Interpersonal skills can be described as how we get along with others on a one-on-one basis. Interpersonal skills can also include active listening, nonverbal communication, and what type of care we show for our subordinates. Regardless of what level we interact with people, we need effective interpersonal skills. One of the things that troubles me the most is when I am not able to get along with everyone. A friend told me that I have an issue with reciprocation. I expect everyone to treat me the way that I treat them and that's true, right? But maybe I have been a little naive to think that everyone is going to treat you with the same level of respect that you treat them. But there should be an expectation from a subordinate. Just like the heading of this chapter says, "You cannot always choose your subordinates." You are going to have to master the skill of leadership and learn how to get along with everyone.

I broke my own rule when I hired a previous employee. I went on the suggestion of a peer review. That is something that I have never done. When doing my due diligence with hiring quality people I always get in contact with the last manager and see what they say, because they know it all. In this case I hired an employee based on recommendations from friends. If I had been a little bit sharper around the edges, I would have immediately identified that these employees only wanted their friend to come to the site to work with them. What a big mistake that I am continuously being punished for daily. It was evident that this employee was not qualified to do the job they were hired for. They were insubordinate, rude, and stand-offish. Two years after I hired this employee the organization that they oversee is worse than it was when this employee arrived. And I think this is my karma for not sticking to my guns and doing my due diligence by thoroughly vetting a potential employee's qualifications, because there's nothing worse than getting an employee on board who cannot do the job, especially in a fast-paced organization when the opportunity for training does not always present itself.

I openly admit that this happened twice, hiring an employee but realizing when they arrived it was the worst mistake I could have made. Some people are good at interviews, but when they arrive at the job it is a nightmare, so prayer kicked in and I started praying for this situation and I started praying that this employee would produce results. But sometimes that thorn in your side needs to stay there. I always knew things were not going to be unicorns and rainbows. So I look at this employee daily and am constantly reminded of the mistake that I made. I use interpersonal communication skills to try and salvage our relationship for the sake of getting the job done. But sometimes the best tools in your box are useless. So while you cannot always pick your subordinates you can pick the battles you choose to engage in. Every interaction does not have to be a negative interaction. There should be times when the manager and subordinate should be able to come together even if there is a toxic environment.

Two years later, I was in conversation with a colleague from another location. As it happened, this colleague was a previous supervisor of my problematic employee. This previous supervisor ranted and raved about how much of a nightmare this employee was, so I did not feel too bad because there was someone else who could relate regarding this employee. So the best thing we can do now is remain cordial for the sake of the organization. Now there's going to be a time when this employee applies for another job and I am going to be stated as a reference and I plan on being as honest as I can to prevent this from happening to another leader in the future. We just cannot pick the people who work for us if they're already there when we arrive. I believe every relationship is worth salvaging, especially when you try to lead by example. You cannot hold a grudge; you have to let go for the sake of getting the job done. As a leader with acceptable interpersonal skills, I can get along with this employee although I know the disaster that I am dealing with. In today's workforce, employees seem to have more rights than managers. There are EEO complaints, dispute resolution, and all those tools that were put in place to protect the employee, sometimes more than the manager.

In the beginning, realizing that I failed in selecting the right person for the position, I was bitter and angry. I vowed never to take a peer review when it comes to running an organization, which meant finding qualified people. Over the years, too, I felt pity for this employee knowing that if they did not change their attitude, they would never be successful; they would never have an opportunity to grow. I really do believe that some people are committed to being negative. They want to live in that space of negativity; they need to live in that space of negativity. It is what is familiar to them—that's all they know. They cannot survive in any atmosphere other than negativity. I am supposed to train the next generation of leaders, as a leader myself. But sometimes you are going to have to acknowledge your failures. And although we learn from our failures, I believe that some failures are inevitable. I prayed for this employee, prayed for their strength and their professional development. I even prayed that I would be able to deal with this employee on a more positive level, which meant I had to change as well. But at the same time, I had pity on this employee because the core was so bad nothing good could come from this person. I watched and interacted with this person on the most positive and empathetic level that I possibly could. I became a better person while dealing with this person. God will use people to make you better. So instead of complaining and giving the same response of negativity, I became patient and resilient so those little bitty, small digs that this employee put upon me did not matter anymore. One of the hardest things to do is to forgive people who treat you wrong. Our first response is to avoid them like the plague, but what does that do for the relationship? How do you grow? How do they grow? I have learned how to deal with difficult people because I have always believed the way people treat you has nothing to do with you; it is all on them. Can you reflect on that time when, if at all, you had a coworker or employee or someone in your unavoidable circle who was undesirable and ruined the morale of the organization?

Case Study #4:
Tasks Do Not Match the Capacity

Vivian had finally arrived to fill the new position I hired her for. Immediately I realized I had made a big mistake, seeing that she was not the slightest bit qualified. You see, when I hired Vivian, I went against my own rule: Never hire an employee based on a peer review. I disciplined myself to only make calculated decisions based on previous managers' recommendations and not the recommendation of friends. The position Vivian was hired for was not a position that could be taught as you go. There was no time for on-the-job training. Based on the fast pace of the organization, this position required the successor to hit the ground running. However, I dropped my guard for a second and gave in to what I should never have done. People pleasing 101! I wanted to please other employees, so I went against my belief and as a result, the organization suffered. Vivian was rebellious, combative, and refused to be coachable. Although I hired Vivian into the organization, I was not able to reprimand her for her actions. Vivian was in good graces with the head manager, which was not me. Her negative actions were never addressed. When I did try to convey my disapproval of her behavior and performance, it was always reversed to make it look like I had a personal vendetta against her. I quickly realized that influence without authority was my new position. It became embarrassing to know that I brought this unproductive employee into the organization. Do not get me wrong, there were some good ideas Vivian brought to the table when she arrived, but they were never carried out—ideas without execution. If I could add a visual to her actions, I would equate it to the little monkey that beats the cymbals, but quickly runs out of batteries. I did not immediately admit that I failed. I tried my best to work with Vivian. I tried to help her understand how important it was that she took an active role as the leader in her position.

But Vivian was a good manipulator. She was good at portraying herself as the victim. Her insolence and disregard for me as her manager became more aggressive. She would not answer my emails when I tasked her, she would not include me on emails that I should have been on, and she refused to submit required documentation as it pertained to her position. Although I was her manager, my hands were tied. In my organization, and I am sure in many other organizations, employees have more rights than managers. There are several tools in place to protect employees from bad leadership, such as Human Resources, mediation, and in many cases, dispute resolution, and in extreme cases, relocating the employee to another office. I think many employees take this for granted. They see this as an opportunity to continue their bad behavior without consequences.

Several years prior to taking this position, I had an employee who was dishonest about his activities during working hours. Although I had several other employees who needed my attention, it became obvious that most of my time was centered on making sure I knew the exact location of this employee. As a manager, I had to spend countless hours building a case as to why this employee should be reprimanded for committing fraud. As a result of his dishonest behavior, the employee was terminated. In many cases, individuals who are dishonest regarding their time and attendance can remain employed by the organization until they pay the hours back to the employer. I felt no need to stick my neck out for this employee because his behavior became very erratic. And I did not feel it best to vouch for him when he had no remorse for his actions.

Although the circumstances were different between Vivian and my previous employee, the result was the same. The manager's attention is taken away from the organization to focus on repairing the behavior of one employee. But what is the true responsibility of a manager in a scenario such as this? In the first scenario, the influencer without authority is minimized because of a troubled employee. In the second scenario, the influencer was given authority to reprimand a troubled employee. What it all comes down to is remaining influential without authority, and not abusing the level of authority given. Authority is not put in place to abuse or negatively impact an employee, it is put in place to oversee, guide, and direct employees in any capacity they fall under, negative behavior or positive. Regardless of what scenario you face as a leader, your responsibility is to ensure the safety of the organization and the privacy of your workforce.

Chapter 6:
Building a Strong Tribe: Community is Everything

As a leader, it is nearly impossible to escape conflict. On any given day, the expectation should be to make yourself readily available to resolve conflict among personnel. What I have learned is that community is everything. You need a strong support system to get you through. Prayer worked for me; prayer is my support system and prayer has given me hope that I can deal with any difficulty that comes my way. Prayer gives me the discernment to know what people to let in and who not to let in, because not everyone has your best interest in mind. But along with prayer, a community of people who support you and are willing to help you get through tough times is especially important. For me, it has been my best friend of 20-plus years, Lisa Marie Chapin. Lisa and I met at my first duty station in Hawaii. One of the attractive things that first struck me about Lisa was her honesty. Lisa was not afraid to have hard conversations and she was honest when her opinion was requested, which made me think long and hard before I approached Lisa for advice because I knew it would be honest and maybe something that I possibly would not want to hear at the time. I can't say that Lisa and I hit it off instantly, but we had a common interest.

After two years, Lisa was discharged from the Navy, returning to civilian life. Fast forward several years: Lisa is a licensed clinical psychologist and runs a private practice in Denver, Colorado. I guess you can say this is an added benefit of the friendship because all of my therapy sessions are free. And although Lisa specializes in the field of fixing people, I still have to be mindful to not overburden her with my personal issues.

Several years ago, I called upon Lisa to help me through an incredibly stressful conflict I was going through with my supervisor at that time. She was there day and night, talking me through scenarios and basically walking me off the cliff, and I really do appreciate that. I did not take it for granted because I actually implemented her advice and Lisa is not a part of my work organization so there was no bias involved. Some of the scenarios that I shared with her were regarding a variety of people she will never encounter, and it is very unlikely that she would even interact with these people that I am complaining to her about, which made it even better because it allowed her to provide an honest, unbiased opinion.

Lisa and I have been friends for over 20 years and she has seen me at my worst. She has witnessed me climbing and scratching from the pit of Hades to some of the highlights of my personal and professional life, such as starting a non-profit organization that introduced golf to youth and starting a women's athletic clothing brand that designed athletic clothing for plus-sized women. Lisa was supportive when I made the decision to take an assignment in Korea for four years. I remember her saying, "Let's make sure we always stay close." It has been a challenge with the distance, and several time zones, but during the time I was away, we always communicated through social media and we even met up for a vacation in Los Angeles. Another honor badge for our friendship: surviving several time zones. Not everybody is fortunate enough to have a Lisa. To this day, I am thankful that she did not give up on me and has continued to be a rock of my support.

Will and Rochelle have been the strength and the source of my success as a leader. While serving at an organization that was very technical, Will and Rochelle, who were also friends from a previous organization, where we originally met, took me under their wings and showed me the ropes. They arrived in the organization several months before I did, and they were very well rounded on all technical aspects of the organization. I would not have survived the learning curve if it were not for William and Rochelle. They took time to help me understand everything I needed to be successful as a leader. They were very patient, and they were determined to see that I succeeded in that position. To make it more interesting, I was not a part of their leadership chain, as they were contract employees. But they wanted me to succeed and I will be forever grateful for their support. Authority had no role in their willingness to support me. Influence was the winner.

As a leader, I was not intimidated by my need for help, I was new to this environment and needed a crash course in the organizational structure. There is no dishonor in being trained by an employee in a subordinate position. Junior employees are always willing to train leadership. It makes them feel engaged and gives them ownership in the success of the organization by imparting their knowledge on leadership. It was an honor to have been trained by subordinates;

the friendship was the bonus. But friends are not the only support group you can rely on.

Today's definition of a tribe is a group of people with common interests, looking out for each other. That does not mean they all come from the same area. I have heard it said many times that diversity is the key to good support. My minister would always say everyone cannot help you with your problems, so be mindful of who you ask advice from because everybody has not been where you are. Would you ask an electrician how to build a car? Would you ask a librarian for advice on fixing your air conditioner? Not everyone has the answer so be mindful who you enlist as a member of your tribe. I have even confided in coworkers for support. Not that they were necessarily experiencing the same adversity I was or the same issues I was experiencing, but some people just have that servant spirit and they are willing to listen and be supportive with whatever you need. Enlist your tribe members wisely. I have also cried on the shoulders of subordinates. I do not look at rank as a qualification to help me with an issue. Because just like seniors can have certain issues, those who are junior could have experienced the same issue and could possibly be a good resource for support. Family, however, tends to remove all filters when it comes to providing support and advice. Not that brutal honesty is a bad thing, but sometimes you just need a little empathy and a willing ear to speak into. During the funeral for Elijah Cummings, our former President, Barack Obama made a powerful statement. He said, *being a leader does not mean you have to be a punk; being kind and nice to people does not mean you are weak.* Leaders are human too, right? They have bad days and good days like anyone else so if I am having a bad day, I will enlist the support of my tribe members to walk me through a workable solution.

While walking my dog one Saturday morning, I happened to walk by a homeless woman and I said hello and she responded with hello, but I was very intrigued because her English was very perfect. There are many foreigners who speak English, but her English was at the level of what I would hear from a college professor. She enunciated her words perfectly and it was hard to detect her Korean accent. We started talking about art, and she mentioned that she had taught at an art school in New York City. But I did not understand why she was homeless on the streets of Seoul. As we had more interactions I started to learn that she experienced severe burnout. I really believe that being homeless suited her better than dealing with the issues of society. She explained that she tried to work in many other fields but there was always someone out to get her. I believe this thinking was self-inflicted and there might have been some mental issues involved, but I do not judge. I share that interaction because within five seconds of meeting this woman and based on our quick conversation she became a resource that I could vent to when I had a bad day. I would always see her sitting in the homeless community right outside of Seoul station and I would sit and talk with her for several minutes.

I thought it interesting that the upper-class Korean citizens would pass by and wonder why I was sitting talking to this homeless woman. The Bible does say be careful how you treat strangers because you could be entertaining angels in disguise. But we continued to converse with each other for a few months. It seemed like when I passed by the homeless area on my way home from work the soup kitchen where she waited for meals throughout the day would always be open so we would always see each other and I would always look forward to sitting down and speaking with her and just hearing the wisdom that she had to share. It was especially nice talking with her because she had no idea where I worked. She did not know anything about my job. She only knew that I was having problems with certain people in the organization. So her responses were pure and genuine because she had no prior knowledge of my profession. I did not share that story for fame or special attention on how I interact with homeless people; I only shared that story so that it would be clear that what you see on the outside does not determine what's on the inside. I had a friend in high school who had a homeless parent. We would pass by this dingy, unkempt gentleman every day for years and I never knew that was her father. You never know where someone's walk leads them, so just be genuine and kind to everyone you meet, you never know what greatness you will get or what blessing you will get from that interaction. Just be open-minded to giving support and you will be surprised what blessing you receive in the long run.

Chapter 7:
You Cannot Lead from Your Chair

My mentor said, "Let's go do it," not "you go do it."
How powerful when someone says "let's."
– Jim Rohn

How do you call yourself a leader when you never leave your office chair? It baffles me when I attend large organizational events and I hear lengthy speeches from leaders telling their stories of how they spent countless hours mentoring, growing and developing the next generation of leaders, and they did it all sitting behind their desk. An effective leader takes the time to familiarize themselves with individual concerns of each one of their subordinates. This does not mean you have to pry into everyone's business or always micro-manage, but it is good to know something about your subordinates such as their birthday, whether they are married or what hobbies they like to do after work.

From experience in the military, I know how important it is to share about oneself, period. You're on a rotation working 12-hour shifts and you spend time getting to know about each other. During my time in the military, it always made me feel special when the senior enlisted or officers approached me just to ask how I was doing. It made me feel like they were genuinely concerned. It was always easy for them to get whisked away into some meeting or to some urgent situation, but when someone higher in rank with more authority took the time to take an interest in my personal life, I felt empowered. It made me want to do my best. It made me want to work harder for my organization because I knew somebody was concerned for me. I believe it is a requirement to become familiar with the personal lives and interests of your subordinates. I have seen leaders close their office door during the day and pull rank when they want escalated services. I have even seen leaders block themselves from office traffic by raising their computer monitors so they cannot see anyone. I do not see how this behavior encourages good leadership if they know they are intentionally being separated from their leader.

I remember being assigned to an office and the site chief did not even know where the junior personnel sat. One of our higher tenured employees was transferring to another location. The office decided to buy a going-away gift and a cake as a celebration. We invited the site leader to say a few words in the back office where this employee sat, and he walked right past the office without even knowing where it was. He had been in that position for three years and didn't even know where junior personnel sat. That kind of raised an eyebrow because it was evident that he made no effort and showed no interest in learning about junior personnel. Now sometimes, we try and make an excuse by saying, "Oh, he is the top person in the organization; he does not have time to do this or does not have time to do that." He does not answer the trouble tickets, he does not get the 3:00 AM phone calls for service, so why can he not learn more about those individuals who do get those phone calls and who do answer those middle of the night trouble tickets?

Does being a self-proclaimed introvert give this top leader a pass for not interacting with his subordinates? If you are an introvert why would you put yourself in the position to oversee others? But I have also discovered some people who are put in positions of leadership really do not want to be there, period. Sometimes it is a hierarchical structure where you're automatically put in a place of leadership without prior agreement.

As an extrovert I believe in up-close and personal. I like to interact with my subordinates. I enjoy learning about their personal lives hearing about their weekend, and just getting a sense of what goes on in their daily lives. Although I am not the head manager in the organization, I really do believe my influence has impacted the lives of many of my subordinates. Now it was mentioned earlier that influence without authority is ineffective. However, I let my light shine despite my lack of authority. You never know what impact you can have on a person's life just by being kind, by saying hello or just by smiling, which can be infectious.

I remember serving in one office several years ago which was majority military. There was one military service member who was preparing for retirement, and it made me feel good when he said, "You are an exceptionally good listener." I ran with that because he never said, "You tell us what to do all the time" or "you're watching over us all the time." He said I was a very good listener and I took that to heart and always vowed to include that in my leadership style. Because I believe that if you are not listening, you're not learning. There's plenty of work to be done and I know some leaders get inundated with the day-to-day activities of the office, but it is important to make time for junior personnel. You never know who is watching you or who you have influence over.

There was a young lady who worked in my office several years ago and she appeared to be very productive when it came to her daily work role. She was always planning meetings, she was always visiting other locations, and she was definitely putting in work during her time in the office. Upon further investigation it was determined that this employee spent so much time working she never was able to respond to management requirements. This employee had several subordinates under her and although her workload was heavy, she proved herself to be very ineffective because when you are too busy working for yourself, you tend to forget about others. And the reason the term ineffective was mentioned was because this employee had other responsibilities she needed to do in the office but she never was able to finish her responsibilities, because she spent so much time behind her desk, she completely ignored every other task to the point that she became ineffective. I never thought that was possible, to work too much, to the point where you are not doing anything for anyone else. Well, I had a firsthand look at how you can bury yourself so far in your work that you ignore everything else, and you are no real use to the organization if you cannot take care of others.

Case Study #5:
You Only Need a Few

How many interpersonal relationships can one person effectively manage? How many interpersonal interactions do you need on a daily basis to feel confident in your leadership abilities? There was an article that came out in *The New York Times* stating that many elderly residents of assisted living facilities only interact with humans once a week. I found this puzzling, as I interact with people on a daily basis. If the mind is not interacting, the mind is not functioning. With regard to leadership, you do not need a large fan base of hundreds of people to be successful, especially in leadership. Too many chiefs and not enough Indians is a means of distraction and counterproductivity. As a leader in my organization, over time, I was able to identify those select few individuals that I was able to truly rely on. Yeah, there were other employees, but only a few rang out as those I could truly rely on. In my observation, too many hands in the pot ruins the recipe. So in order for me to be successful as a leader, I seek out those employees who appear to be the most intuitive, the hardest-charging and the most committed to their personal growth. It is a small organization but the individuals who are considered my "go-to" employees contribute to my success as a leader.

When I was in the military, one of my first leadership positions was a watch section supervisor. Each watch section was made up of seven to ten individuals. These individuals ranged from serving their first year in the military to senior enlisted. I did not need all of them to perform one task. I sought out that hard-charging individual who set himself above the rest. I sought out the individuals who were always on time and always showed a genuine interest in progress. Now I did have others on my team who obviously were only there because it was a part of their job responsibility. They showed no enthusiasm or interest in their work in the slightest sense. As a leader, leading by example was not always effective, especially with those individuals who had no interest in the job. What do you do? How do you motivate the unmotivated? So to make the job successful for everyone, I rallied those few individuals and explained to them how their contribution and support were central to the success of the organization. I edified them. I pumped them up. I gave them a sense of ownership and empowerment. And this helped them understand the importance of getting the job done.

As a leader the most essential part of growing people is empowerment and edification. You have to give people a sense of entitlement. They have to feel like they belong and that they are a valuable asset to the organization. The other individuals had no interest in empowerment or edification. They were just "hitchhikers," looking for a ride to the next opportunity. I didn't treat them any differently than the "passengers," the personnel who were in it for the long haul. I had to see them for what they were. The "hitchhikers" had no issue with this; they only wanted to be told what to do, given a script to follow. Not everyone is interested in leadership, so I did not hold it against them. I ensured that my trusted few provided them with clear direction, clear instructions, and clear guidance on what was expected from them on a daily basis. And it worked because I did not need to manage 30 people. I managed the leadership skills of 10 people who managed the personal growth of everyone else.

But on the other side of that coin, there are some leaders who gather the information on their own. They do not feel like they need additional people to help them and I have seen situations where some leaders feel that they're better off doing all the work themselves, but what does this do for the people that are expected to come behind them as leaders? What does it do for the future managers, the future subordinates, who are expected to take charge when we move on? You cannot do everything on your own; you simply cannot do everything. You have to share information and you have to be willing to share the workload. The biggest reason for attrition in some organizations is the lack of leadership and lack of opportunity. As mentioned before, people do not leave jobs, they leave people. If you are not growing people for success you are not leading. Today a friend mentioned that the goal of a leader is not to be in charge; rather, the goal of a leader is to care for those who are in your charge. That resonated with me because I have always been mindful of making sure that I am setting the best example as a leader. I have not been able to please everyone, but I think I have a good track record of pleasing a few. My advice to any new leader would be to rally around those individuals who show a genuine interest in leading. You cannot invest time and energy in those who are not willing to learn, willing to lead, and most important, those who are not willing to be coachable. Being a leader is not for cowards. It takes communication, it takes patience, and it takes follow-through.

David was an incredibly talented and thorough project lead; he gained the respect of every employee under his authority. David was an influencer because he knew the projects inside and out. However, David was not in an official leadership capacity. David enjoyed working with people and learning about the projects he oversaw, but David refused to take an official leadership position. David was able to shine without authority; however, when you took a closer look at David's role it was obvious that he did not have the qualities of a leader. I would say David was a good team lead, at best. Although David had authority and influence over his team, he eventually proved himself to be inefficient. You might ask how David could have influence over his team but still be inefficient. Let me explain it to you: David had several team members who worked under him. David took on a lot of responsibility; at times his plate was overflowing, which created a sense of being overwhelmed. As a ripple effect, David did not answer requirements from leadership, David did not attend important meetings that he was asked to attend. Leadership began to notice and questioned his ability to multitask. David was a high-ranking employee. At his level he was expected to delegate to his team. But David was ineffective in his performance because he was unable to meet management requirements and spent too much time fielding requirements that should have been delegated to his team.

This is something I have realized many times: People can be high performing but at the same time ineffective, depending on what tasks they are performing. As a leader, I noticed the junior ranking employees are the most determined. They're hungry to get to the next level so they tend to work harder than a complacent senior ranking official who has no aspirations to advance any farther than where they already are. For this reason, I believe in giving junior employees the opportunity to lead in an organization because of their ability to bring newer ideas.

Chapter 8:
Influence vs. Authority

We make a living by what we get;
we make a life by what we give.
– Winston Churchill

Influence is the ability to gain favor from subordinates, peers, and colleagues based on the positive energy conveyed or resonated. How do you gain or achieve influence? As an influencer, what should your followers see in you that will benefit them? As an influencer, your purpose is to meet the emotional and inspirational needs of your supporters or influence benefactors; you have to tell a great story that someone needs to hear. As an influencer, I seek to improve the experience for everyone I interact with. Mainly, just being myself without reservation works best. Vulnerability, empathy, and integrity are key to an influencer's productivity. Instead of leading by fear, I choose to lead by influence. Of course, fear works for a leader and is sometimes the best approach, depending on your environment. Employees will do whatever is asked or demanded of them out of worry for job security, but which approach will improve the quality of an employee's productivity? Showing up ready to jump in is a great attribute of an influencer. What better opportunity to display sovereignty than to be a working leader rather than a watching leader?

I was invited to speak at a Vision Board Party on Camp Casey Army base in Dongducheon-si, South Korea. The purpose of the vision board event was to encourage young soldiers and family members to remain resilient during emotionally challenging periods of their careers. A recent command climate survey revealed that the third most prevalent area of concern for military personnel is a lack of leadership. It was revealed that soldiers who do not trust their subordinates will provide adequate support during challenging times. More soldiers felt that their leadership contributed to their stress on a daily basis, more than helped to resolve stress. As a result of negative leadership, there have been reports of increased spousal abuse, excessive debt, poor work performance, and adverse behavior in the workplace. As families are being separated by deployments, training exercises, and other requirements of the uniform, it is easy for service members and their families to experience stress and anxiety, not to mention challenges that accompany starting a career in the military at a lower rank or lack of authority. My topic of discussion was Influence vs. Authority.

In 2019, 57% of employees quit their jobs because of toxic bosses. Let that sink in for a second—more than half the workforce sought employment elsewhere because of negative people. There is an old saying, "People do not leave jobs; they leave people." If an opportunity to transition does not immediately present itself, Mahatma Gandhi says, "Be the change you want to see." Dr. Phil followed up by saying, "You must teach people how to treat you." How does this tie into influence and authority? It has been proven that the majority of influencers in an organization are not in a position of authority.

Seventeen-year-old Greta Thunberg, a student from Stockholm, Sweden, staged a school protest in support of addressing climate change. At the age of 15 she convinced her parents to make small changes that would reduce the carbon footprint in their household. In an effort to take her cause a bit further, Greta started holding up signs in front of her school advocating for climate change. What do you think happened soon after? Other students in her school and neighboring schools began to rally behind her, and as a result, the infamous "Fridays for the Future" movement was created, where students around the world would strike on Fridays in support of climate change. Greta's conviction led to action that gained her influence. To date, there are over four million participants in the Fridays for the Future movement. Greta went on to speak at the 2018 United Nations Climate Change conference and was also selected as Time Magazine's person of the year in 2019. Greta was not a member of her student body council; she was not the class president; she was a young lady with conviction on something she wanted to see changed. She acted on her intuition and because of that, others followed suit and she became a national icon for climate change with no authority whatsoever. She became an influencer who had the courage to speak out against something she felt very passionate about.

Jaden Smith, the son of Will and Jada, responded to the urgent water contamination crisis that killed 12 people, caused brain damage to hundreds of children, and sickened many others in Flint, Michigan. With no authority whatsoever, Jaden responded to a national crisis. Teaming with a local nonprofit organization and other local members of the Flint community, in addition to using his own funds, he used his influence to create the infamous "Water Box" that allows 10 gallons of water to be micro filtered within 60 seconds, allowing Flint residents access to hundreds of gallons of bacteria-free water in minutes. At that time, the city of Flint had no clean drinking water for over 1700 days. Jaden was not a member of the Flint community, nor was he from the state of Michigan, but he led with influence. Jaden had a conviction that led to action that gained him influence. The authority figures for the city of Flint have since changed, but the influence of Mr. Smith will live on for generations.

As a senior level manager, I can relate to having influence without authority. When I first arrived in Korea in 2016, I was under the purview of a really great leader. He allowed me to learn my job in peace. He did not micromanage me. He did not dictate my actions. He trusted me to do the job he hired me to do. His favorite saying was, "Go rookie, and do great things." He allowed me to be the leader that I was intended to be. But 14 months later he transitioned back to the U.S. and what I was left with was nothing good, I will just say that.

In what felt like the wink of an eye, my authority was taken from me. I was an executive level manager in the Department of Defense, and without explanation, my authority was taken away from me. I am not sure why it happened, but I know I was left with nothing. However, I still had 30-plus subordinates that I had to lead and manage and guide on a daily basis so I had to reinvent myself. I had to re-create my position to remain relevant. I had to make something that was good for my subordinates. It was a learning opportunity. I could have done better, even though I had my moments of frustration. There was nothing I could have done; I was number two in command. I was not the Chief of the organization, I was the Deputy Chief, and when you are in a position of an assistant or a deputy, sometimes your great ideas only go as far as what your Chief thinks. You can be the most creative and the most talented person, but if those in authority do not feel that way then you are lost in translation. But what I did have was the influence I created and the relationships I nourished from the beginning, so when I needed that influence, it was right there waiting for me.

I transitioned from Korea eventually and I had another group of subordinates. I had another opportunity to influence. There was another authority figure, but what I knew now was how to deal with difficult people and how to remain present for my subordinates. It was not easy, but I had to overcome adversity. I was not the same person I was when I arrived. I was more mature. I had a better relationship with God and my prayer life had improved.

I am still not perfect and I will never be perfect but, what I am, is an influencer with limited authority. So, my charge for you today is to mentor, empower, create, and bring up, because one thing you need to know is that your behavior is emulated and what is emulated is repeated. I must say that again: Your behavior is emulated, and what is emulated is repeated—good or bad. So what are you passing down as an influencer? What are you creating? What type of impression are you making on your workforce? Be the change that you want to see because I was the change that I wanted to see.

Let me share my rationale on why influence outperforms authority. Now, I am not dinging authority figures here today; that is not the intention of my message, because we all have been in a position where we reported to someone higher than ourselves. We have all been in a position where we wanted to express our great ideas and perspectives but might not be in the position of authority to implement those great ideas. Right? So, here we go...

The first thing you should understand is that it is possible to be the lowest ranking person in the room but have the most influence. You might ask yourself how anyone can be influenced by a private or an airman. Well, influence is not about the rank you wear; influence is about how you make people feel. Lisa Haisha, Motivational Speaker and Coach, explained, "Great leaders do not set out to be a leader...they set out to make a difference. It is never about the role; it is always about the goal." Authority is only temporary; it is based on a position. Authority is deliberate and intentional. If you are in a position of authority, here is a great way to assess your leadership proficiency. Call a former subordinate and invite them for lunch. If they show up, you have made an impact. If they do not, there's your assessment. Whose life have you changed? Whose life have you made better? Keep in mind, people do not follow you because you tell them to; they follow you because you inspire them to. As a junior subordinate, you can make an impact by creating opportunities for others. Be that guy or girl who inspires subordinates you have purview over. Coach! Mentor! Empower! Be empathetic! That is how you outlast authority; be someone's success story. As an authoritative figure and influencer, my goal is to always improve the experience of my subordinates. Since you are required to share space and time with your subordinates and colleagues, you might as well improve their experience, so why not seek to improve your experience as well?

How you show up is always a choice. In this military environment someone is always watching you, someone is always learning from you. Junior personnel emulate; they are very impressionable. Someone will always be influenced by your behavior, regardless if it is good or bad. As an E-5 in the Navy, I spent a lot of time on the watch floor. The watch floor was an extraordinarily complex place. Many things happened that were unpredictable. There was a Watch Officer who oversaw all functions during the 12-hour shift. The watch team consisted of maybe seven or eight personnel. Now, before I was promoted to the position of Watch Officer, I was a junior team member. The Watch Officer at the time was a very high-strung Navy Chief who lacked interpersonal skills and was verbally abusive to junior personnel. However, he was in a position of authority, so whatever the Chief instructed, everyone went along with. But because of the way he used his authority, he lacked the ability to influence. He missed an opportunity to mentor and retain the interest of junior personnel serving in the military. During his tour on command, he intimidated and led with fear. His assessment of his ability to lead resulted in minimum participation to reserve an event room for his going-away event. If you cannot get five people to show up at your farewell event, what does that say about your leadership ability? Well, to me, it says you are not a leader at all.

I read an article that said, "People are inspired to perform their best, not driven to perform." I thank you for the opportunity today to share my thoughts on influence and authority. My name is Jeanette Ortegon, I am a Manager and today I thank you for the opportunity to speak, inspire and love. Thank you.

Case Study #7:
Speak Up! You Have
Everything to Lose

Have you ever found yourself in a situation where you noticed something was not right, but you were afraid to speak up? If you answered yes to that question, you will learn from someone who did just the opposite. Julia was a member of the repair team and found herself in the same situation. Julia was a line supervisor responsible for ensuring all repairs in the toy division were completed accurately. Julia was responsible for ensuring all toys were ready to be sold off the shelf without the possibility of product returns. Julia was a remarkable employee. She did everything to ensure her job was done right, without the normal shortcuts that other employees would slide in. Julia was amazed that upper management did not catch on to the shortcuts that were being practiced on other teams.

Julia did a great job steering clear of negativity. She knew she was on her own when her supervisor refused to help her report discrepancies she witnessed on other teams. After further research, Julia discovered that her immediate supervisor was encouraging members of her team to take the same shortcuts in order to meet deadlines. Julia kept this information to herself and she also kept her integrity by ensuring that all products were thoroughly inspected for defects. She was not the most favored person in the organization because Julia reported all defective products instead of allowing them to be sold off the shelf in a degraded condition. Julia was fed up with the fraudulent behavior of the organization and decided to report her supervisor to the next line of leadership. Julia became even more frustrated when the next line supervisors did not take her seriously. Instead of investigating Julia's claim, they allowed the behavior to continue.

Julia felt it was best if she were to transfer from her immediate supervisor's team into a team that followed ethical practices. Her request was denied. It appeared Julia's supervisor had influence over the entire department, including regional headquarters, located hundreds of miles away. Julia's supervisor had a reputation of imposing fear and intimidation upon anyone who stood in his way.

Julia had many sympathizers, but none who were willing to stick their necks out and publicly show support for her. Julia's supervisor was suspected of being a racist based on the way he treated African American employees in the organization. However, there was not enough clear evidence that anyone would report to substantiate such claims. Julia felt alienated and betrayed. She could not wrap her mind around the fact that everyone in her chain of command knew there were defects in many products but still allowed them to be sold. Julia did the right thing by reporting this fraudulent behavior to the next line of leadership, but she was completely oblivious as to why she was ignored.

What would you have done in Julia's case? Julia was only a team lead, which meant her influence was trumped by her lack of authority. Julia was not in a position to quit her job; she had been with the company for 20-plus years and was looking forward to retiring within the next 10 years. Julia continuously reported the negative behavior to leadership, which eventually paid off. They finally decided to assist Julia with moving to another team. Julia finally felt like her patience and persistence were properly addressed. However, when Julia's supervisor was notified that Julia would be leaving the team, he intimidated upper leadership into retracting their proposal to relocate Julia. Julia was devastated. *How could leadership ignore my concern and throw me to the wolves?* she nervously pondered, realizing she had nowhere else to turn.

Ironically, there was an audit in her division scheduled for the following month. In the meantime, Julia had to walk the hallways in shame until the audit, which was her opportunity to report the negative behavior to an outside source. Julia's supervisor taunted her because she was forced to work for him under his terms and conditions. Julia was furious that she was powerless and all alone. She anticipated the day she would be able to tell her story to the auditors. Leadership had no idea Julia had a plan to report what she had been experiencing. They were unaware that she would be reporting her immediate supervisor and everyone in her leadership chain, including the top senior executive of her organization.

In the interim, Julia did her job with dignity and grace although she was shamed by employees and leadership for what they perceived as losing the battle to relocate out of the division. She continued to serve her subordinates although her level of authority quickly dwindled as a repercussion of reporting her fraudulent supervisor. Julia made a big decision when reporting her supervisors to the audit team. She knew this would put her in a tough situation at work. She took a risk. But what did Julia really have to lose? She was a leader, although a leader without authority; she was still in a position to influence subordinates. What did she really have to lose? She was not respected by anyone in the chain of command. No one took her seriously when she reported her supervisor for retaliation.

What would you have done in Julia's circumstances? As you read this case, what are your thoughts on where you stand as a leader or a subordinate? Did Julia have other options? It was previously stated that she was not able to give up her career. She felt the best thing for both parties would have been to relocate out of her dysfunctional division into a more controlled division that supported her desire for integrity. Do you think Julia should have resigned from the company? What do you think her leadership deserved for ignoring Julia's concerns and retaliating against her for reporting fraud and abuse?

Julia eventually got her opportunity to report the continuous retaliation and abuse to the auditors. Julia peacefully anticipated the day her supervisor would be held accountable for his abusive and negligent actions. To date, Julia is still waiting to receive justice. Maybe she never will. This might be one of those situations that Julia will only learn from. If you learn anything from Julia, you will learn to expose your bullies. Everyone answers to someone. Even the authority has an authority figure. Julia looked around many times and there was no one to support her except her courage and her own determination. God is always in the mix. And maybe this is what Julia needed to become a better manager. I'm sure other opportunities will allow her to use the training in this situation. Nothing is wasted; nothing evolves without purpose. Everything happens for a reason and everything prepares us for our future assignment, regardless of whether it's in a professional setting, a personal setting, or anything in life. What we're doing today prepares us for what's next to come and Julia really understood that. Do not allow yourself to be taken advantage of—report wrongdoing without a negative reaction or retaliation.

Julia finally departed from the organization without hesitation from anyone, obviously, because her moral character and Christian beliefs were not welcomed or viewed as a necessity. It was actually looked upon as a distraction because Julia always displayed her love for God, even in the presence of nonbelievers. And to her surprise, individuals were watching her amazing work ethic. They were paying attention to the way she handled conflict and to the way she stood up for subordinate employees. Julia was offered a better position with another organization. Julia happily accepted the position but was surprised when the individual who interviewed her mentioned that he could not find one person to say anything bad about her. Everybody enjoyed her personality and appreciated her enthusiasm and love for every project they worked on with her. Julia was in disbelief. She was so heartbroken based on the way she was treated at her previous organization she never imagined being offered this position. That goes to show anyone that if you work hard and don't retaliate or do grimy things to hurt people, the opportunity makers are watching, and the opportunities will be limitless.

Chapter 9:
Calculated Approach to Slaying the Dragon

At this point, it should be clear that influence is a bonus as a result of leadership in the absence of authority. I've given my testimony of what leadership means to me: It means making an impact in someone's life, setting an example that would make a positive difference to others. I spent many years as a subordinate, and I had a chance to witness firsthand some of the worst leaders imaginable. I have seen military careers ended because of negative leadership. I have seen what stress can do as a result of bad leaders and I can't imagine how these leaders get away with making negative impacts on innocent lives. That's only because the top has gotten so high, they can't see that far down. But in my experience, I have learned how to slay the dragon. I'll leave you with a few tips that work for me.

I never resort to verbal abuse. I never retaliate. I never play tit for tat. Those kinds of strategies create tension rather than resolve conflict.

I'm not defined by where I started. I started at a place where it was not easy to speak up for myself, but I learned along the way that guarding my mental health was my responsibility.

Negative things are going to happen to you; that's one thing you cannot escape. I mentioned earlier that God allows us to experience things only to make us stronger for circumstances that we will face in the future. Attribute your training to God's providence.

Something else I've learned about being a strong leader is using what you have in front of you. And what that means is using all available resources that are present and available to you. This could be hardworking employees, office allies, subordinate personnel— any resource that's willing to help you strive to be a better leader and to achieve career goals. The successful leader always has an ally, someone not necessarily in the same office but someone who is there to provide support whenever needed.

I remember an assignment to a particular office several years ago, where we had limited resources. No relationships were created in order to get the job done effectively. Although I can't publicly speak about what their job was, it really relied on making relationships with people. I immediately noticed everyone making phone calls or sending emails, but no one got up and walked over to another location to meet the individuals they needed support from. As I mentioned earlier in the book that I was very good at making relationships and creating relationships that never existed and that still exist although I've been gone for several years. An exceptional leader will always do well in creating relationships.

I would always tell my son, "You can be an example, or you can learn from examples." I hope he remembers it is more important that he learn from examples rather than become an example.

As leaders we learn from mistakes, but mistakes will make less sense until we learn from them. I can honestly say that my mistakes have been some of my greatest lessons that I have learned from. But the greatest mistake that I've learned as a leader was to accept rejection. I work very hard for my managers and when I'm not appreciated, I feel empty. I feel hopeless. And this is only because as a subordinate you can only watch when things go wrong. There's very little you can do without buy in from your supervisor. But I've always learned to stay true to myself; in my despair I remained who I am. I never minimized. I never watered my beliefs down to make someone else feel comfortable, because I've always believed the way people treat you has nothing to do with you. They've treated everyone in the same manner. You're just a passerby who happens to be impacted by their behavior.

Stand up for yourself; never let someone destroy you. You might be the only one on the island but at least you remain true to yourself. People are watching your behavior, especially in a position of leadership. Relationships could be made or broken when you spend one minute out of character. Pray to God continuously. As a leader maintain a strong prayer life not only for yourself but for your employees and leadership. Pray and know that God is listening. This journey is yours to own. No one can take it from you. I wish you much success in your leadership endeavors. I wish you much success in your prayer life. I hope this account of how I lead by influence will be instrumental in your life as a leader. Be blessed.

www.ingramcontent.com/pod-product-compliance
Lightning Source LLC
Chambersburg PA
CBHW072210270326
41930CB00011B/2606